I'M PUZZLED!
Who Moved My Pieces?

by Dr. Kevin B. Lee

I'M PUZZLED!
Who Moved My Pieces?

by Dr. Kevin B. Lee

© Copyright 2018 KBL Ministries

ISBN-13:
978-1732139909 (Dr. Kevin B. Lee)

ISBN-10:
1732139903

Dr. Kevin B. Lee

Dedication

This book is dedicated to the vast number of children and youth workers who tirelessly give of their time, talent, and treasure.

Words cannot adequately express my deepest admiration of the invaluable time that you give weekly, monthly, and yearly to encourage young people in their walk with God.

Thank you for helping young people with their salvation. A personal relationship with God through Jesus Christ is so vital for children and youth today.

Thank you for assisting young people in growing spiritually in their walk with God.

Thank you for serving young people as they discover their purpose in the kingdom God.

Special Thanks

I want to give special thanks to the following individuals who have assisted me in completing my fifth book.

I give special thanks to my patient and beautiful wife Karen. She gives of herself so that I can fulfill my call to ministry. Baby, I thank God for you every day.

I praise God for the Staff and Berean Christain Church family in Gwinnett County. What an awesome privilege to pastor faithful and loving people who pray for and follow their shepherd.

Thanks to my "G-Men" brothers who fasted with me while I tarried in finishing this book.

Dr. Kevin B. Lee

Acknowledgements

Special thanks to Leslie E. Royal who was so instrumental in helping me to publish this book. I'm not sure if I would have sucessfully completed this book without her persistence, excellence, and expertise.

Special thanks to all of my editors who worked tirelessly to help me meet my deadlines. Thanks for all of those extra eyes and hours you sacrificed so that this book could impact all those who read it. (Mother Thelma Lee, Mother Relia Lee, and Dr. Armada Pinkins)

Special, special shout-out to Sister Tammy Parker-Outley and Principal Andrea Mitchell who spent countless hours in writing and editing. I was able to see the light at the end of the tunnel because of their faithfulness and steadfastness!

To God be the glory for His majesty and mercy. To God be the glory for His grace and favor. To God be the glory for He never stops loving us or forgetting about us!

Table of Contents

Chapter 1: Structuring the Ministry ....,.... 1

Chapter 2: Keeping the Ministry from
Crumbling 16

Chapter 3: Using Outreach to Build Ministry ... 32

Chapter 4: Recruiting Volunteers 43

Chapter 5: Retaining Volunteers 60

Dr. Kevin B. Lee

Introduction

Have you ever been puzzled by what you need to do in order to have continued success in Children and Youth Minstry? Have you ever been puzzled about how some ministries accomplish and maintain growth with success in their children and youth departments? Is it their leadership? Is it the budget? Is it the workers or the resources? Sometimes it is just a puzzle trying to find the answers to what makes children and youth ministry work.

This book, *"I'M PUZZLED! Who Moved My Pieces"*, will give you some practical tools that will help you unlock answers to questions that have stagnated your Children and Youth Ministry.

Take your time, read and glean helpful knowledge and proven skills on how to transform your ministry into actions benefiting children and youth.

Chapter 1

Structuring My Ministry

"Every church, whether big or small, should start with some structure."
Author Unknown

Structure is a vital piece in establishing a Children and Youth Ministry. The dictionary defines structure as the mode of building, constructing or organizing. In working with children and youth, structure helps to build a well organized ministry in which your church can be proud. Structure gives direction and clarity for the ministry, so that the guessing of ministry success is eliminated.

The Definition of Children & Youth Ministry
Children's Ministry is **intentional planning** that seeks to primarily meet the spiritual needs of young people from the 1st through the 5th grade.

Youth Ministry is ***intentional planning*** that seeks to primarily meet the spiritual needs of young people from the 6th through the 12th grade. Notice how I divided up the Children and Youth Ministry. The Children's Ministry focus is the 1st through the 5th grade. The Youth Ministry focus is on the 6th through the 12th grade.

The reason that I chose this model to departmentalize is because this is what most schools utilize in their systems. Elementary school is for children in the 1st through the 5th grade. Middle and high school are for 6th through 12th grade students. Many churches subscribe to dividing their ministry by age. Either way is fine. However, you should determine what works best for you and your ministry. Breaking young people up by ages is beneficial. However, sometimes breaking them up by grades is advantageous as well. Whatever you do is okay. That is, as long as you demonstrate flexibility and remember that you are seeking to reach and meet the needs of the young people.

Pay close attention to the words intentional progamming. A structured ministry for young people should be methodical as well as practical rather than whimsical or lackadaisical. A ministry characterized by lack of order or planning is headed for trouble. Aimless and arbitrary planning creates an environment that is not conducive for young people to growing spiritually. Young people need ministries that plan a program with a purpose. Parents are seeking churches where they know their children can grow spiritually. Parents appreciate organized and nurturing environments where their children can mature in the Word of God.

Notice I said, **spiritual** needs are primary. There are a plethora of other needs that leaders should address. However, the spiritual is most important. They must learn about God and His love for them and the world. Young people must know about the perfect Jesus Christ who is the Savior of the world. They must learn the role that the Holy Spirit plays in their lives as believers. Children should not grow up in our ministries ignorant about God's Word. It is a sad indictment on our ministry when the Bible is not central and dominant in the classroom. Teaching young people how to mature in their walk and live a life of discipleship is our foremost goal in ministry.

Other needs you should consider are relational, emotional, mental and physical. I want to address the relational and emotional needs. It is a known fact that young people need relationships. They grow through and by relating with one another. When you talk about relationships, you are talking about the association or connection between people. Young people desire to feel connected to those who lead them. That means you! They don't relish teachers who want them to know the WORD only. They relish teachers that want to know them personally.

Remember the old saying, "Young people don't care how much you know until they know you care about them." (something like that) Oh I have it now, *"Kids don't care how much you know until they know how much you care."* Get to know your students' names, parents, hobbies, likes, dislikes, struggles, favorite classes, friends they hang with, issues they struggle with, music they listen to, who they date, etc. (You get the picture.) We can't get so hung up on the spiritual that we miss out on the relational.

As a matter of fact, it is the relational component that helps us to connect the spiritual. Thank God for Jesus coming so that we could have a personal relationship with the Father. What the law could not do in the Old Testament, Jesus did in the New Testament. Also, young people have emotional needs that are crucial. They have feelings of joy, sorrow, fear, hate, love, etc. We must ask the Holy Spirit how to meet these needs.

We must ask the Holy Spirit to show us the emotional needs of our young people. Their needs may change daily, weekly, monthly or quarterly. Determining how young people's needs are affecting them is challenging. Thank God for James 1:5a, "If any man lacks wisdom, let him ask God who gives generously." Start asking God for wisdom.

The Destination of Children & Youth Ministry
When providing structure for the ministry, there are some vital components necessary. Listed below are components needed for structure in a Children and Youth Ministry.

1. **Adult Core Team**
   The adult core team is mainly comprised of five to seven individuals who work with the children and youth. They are involved in the day to day operations of the ministry. These workers function in various roles in the ministry and pretty much know the strengths and weaknesses of the ministry. This adult core team is extremely passionate about the work and has a strong desire to see success in the ministry. These leaders communicate with each other several times a week and come together monthly to plan, discuss needs, and evaluate the health of the ministry.

2. **Adult Leaders**
   This group is comprised of adults who work directly with children and youth. Their role is to volunteer to work in some aspect of the ministry. They may or may not have an interest in the total programming of the ministry. They fulfill their role and keep it moving. They should meet at least quarterly to discuss and participate in the evaluation of the ministry.

3. Youth Leadership Council

This group is an assembly of young people made up of middle and high school students. These students possess a sincere heart for God and serve as mini assistants to the adult leaders. They serve examples to their peers and their duties are to help plan and implement programs. The value of their presence and voice demonstrates the importance of inclusiveness when structuring ministries. Peers can share in the selection of the youth council or they can be selected by the adults in the ministry. A good team consist of three to seven youth depending on the size of your youth ministry. They meet monthly with the youth director or adult core team to help with evaluation, development and implementation of programs.

4. Leadership Team

This group is comprised of a group of young people who are not serving on the youth council. However, they too demonstrate a heart of service and seek to make an impact within the ministry. This group is optional, depending on the size of your ministry. The middle school group can serve in this role while your high schoolers serve on the youth council. Or you may choose to have just one of the two groups. The key is for you to continue praying about and discovering what works best for your ministry.

5. Parenting Team
This team is comprised of parents who desire to see the ministry succeed. They are invested in the ministry and are passionate about excellence and growth. They have bought into the vision and willingly serve to support and oversee specific committees to help ensure success. These components can provide the added support needed to structure your ministry for success. Pray and ask God to lead you in adding all or some of these components to your ministry.

The Dedication of Children & Youth Ministry
Experiencing success in the ministry will have a lot to do with your dedication. What you devote yourself to will determine the outcome and success. Listed below are several recommendations for structuring a Children and Youth Ministry.

1. **Look** for the Right People
As you search for the volunteers, parents, youth council, and leadership teams, you should commit to finding the right people. Everybody who desires to serve in ministry is not right for ministry or sometimes not ready for the work. Having the right people in place will make a huge difference. The right people can enhance and elevate the ministry to the next level. However, the wrong people can hinder and stifle the ministry. It is

always good to establish qualifications and expectations when looking for the right people.

2. **Learn** from the Right People
    There are a variety of ministries, organizations and people that can serve as a model of inspiration for you. Having a good model to see and follow enhances your effectiveness. There are ministries, organizations and people in your community that can assist you in gaining insight that benefit the ministry. Don't be afraid to step out of your comfort zone to learn from others. Some of your greatest blessings will come from outside of your church.

3. **Leverage** from the Right People
    One definition of the word leverage means the power or ability to influence people, events, or decisions. You will need leverage in youth ministry. Who in your church has the ability to influence people? You will benefit from knowing people with power and influence that can persuade the church to see the need to invest in Children and Youth Ministry. The same holds true for the community. Look for businesses, organizations or persons outside the church that can provide resources to expand your work within the church.

4. **Lean** on the Right People

One definition for lean is to rest against or on something for support. Another definition for lean is to depend or rely upon someone or something. Leaning on the right people will help you mentally, physically and emotionally. There is nothing like good strong solid people that provide needed support and experience. Sometimes it is mentally, physically and emotionally draining ministering to young people. When these areas are affected, it will ultimately challenge you spiritually. A depleted youth leader can only go so far before there is burnout! Ask God to send you some Timothys and Silases to do the work He has called you to do.

The Implementation of Children & Youth Ministry

This section is designed to share some key points when beginning new ministries or trying to build on something already established.

1. Discuss with your Senior Pastor

Your senior pastor needs to know everything you are planning for the ministry. Nothing should ever catch him or her off guard. Make sure there is nothing hidden from him or her. Some pastors are very hands on while others seem to allow the ministry to flow from a distance.

2. Devote to Prayer

Prayer must become a priority for a succesful ministry. You cannot make it without prayer and the power of the Holy Spirit. The Bible declares in Matthew 7:7, "Ask and it shall be given, seek and you shall find, knock and the door shall be opened." Trust in the promises of God knowing that He will answer all of our prayers according to His will and His timing.

3. Determine Goals and Objectives

Goals are very much needed. Goals give focus and help to give direction. It is imperative that we know the direction of the ministry. Goals also give clarity. They help us to see what we desire and what the end results should and could look   like. Objectives are the means that help us find our way toward our goals. The objectives assist us in accomplishing our goals.

4. Define the Need

Meet with adult leaders and youth to discover the primary needs of the ministry. Make sure this is a collaborative effort. Hear thoughts and ideas from the pastor, parents and others connected to the ministry. Identify the top five needs and develop an intentional plan to implement and execute.

5. Develop a Planning Team

Tap into the gifts of your church members. Find someone who plans and   executes well. There is someone in the ministry with the gift of organization and administration. This person may already serve in the youth ministry or may be a member at large. These are valuable gifts that enhance the ministry by taking it to the next level.

6. **Delegate Assignments**
   Make sure one person is not responsible for everything.   Break up assignments into manageable pieces. Try to get as much buy-in as possible. Hopefully, others will not mind taking responsibility for implementation and execution.

7. **Don't Give Up**
   No matter how slow things move or how long it takes progress to take place, make up your mind that you won't give up or give in. A wise pastor once instructed his congregation to tell themselves "I am too tough to quit!" You may become discouraged and daunted, but stay with it! You may grow tired and exasperated, but stay with it! You may feel isolated and alone, but stay with it! Remember Paul's words in I Corinthians 15:57, "Therefore, my beloved brethren, be ye steadfast, unmoveable, always abounding in the work of the Lord, forasmuch you know that your labor is not in vain."

Chapter Reflection

What was the most important thing that God spoke to you?

_____

_____

_____

_____

_____

_____

_____

What did God speak to you about that you would like to implement in the next 30 to 90 days?

_____

_____

_____

_____

_____

_____

_____

What would hinder you from implementing what God spoken has to you in this chapter?

_____

_____

_____

_____

_____

Structuring the Ministry

1. What is the definition of Children and Youth Ministry?

   _____

   _____

2. What are the two key words in the definition?

   _____   _____

3. What is the difference between a Youth Leaders Council and a Youth Leadership team?

   _____

   _____

4. Why is it important to look for the right people when seeking volunteers?

   _____

   _____

5. Who is most important to share ideas with when beginning something new in ministry?

   _____

   _____

6. Why is it important to never give up?

   _____

   _____

   _____

   _____

Chapter Notes

_____

_____

_____

_____

_____

_____

_____

_____

_____

_____

_____

_____

_____

_____

_____

_____

_____

_____

_____

_____

_____

_____

_____

_____

_____

_____

_____

_____

Chapter 2

Keeping the Ministry from Crumbling

*"Anything that continues to crumble
will eventually fall."*
Author Unknown

Have you ever asked yourself, "How do I keep my ministry from crumbling?" In ministry, there are seasons of growth and movement. There are also seasons of very little growth and very little movement. There are so many challenges leaders wrestle with that can cause their ministry to crumble. There are a number of things you can implement to keep your Children and Youth Ministry from decaying and finally dying. I have listed seven important factors to keep your ministry from crumbling.

1. *It Takes PLANNING*

Proverbs 30:25 says, "The ants are people not strong, yet they prepare their meat in the summer." (KJV) This Bible verse helps us to understand the power of planning. The ants, though small creatures, are able to accomplish so much because they plan. It's going to take serious planning in order to keep your ministry from crumbling.

First, establish your direction. Know where you are going! It is impossible to get somewhere if you don't know where you're headed. You should establish the direction you would like to see the ministry moving. Listed below are some suggested goals that you could seek to accomplish in your Children and Youth Ministry.

- Vision from the pastor
- Budget increase
- More youth in Bible Study
- Parental involvement
- Ministerial participation
- More ministry opportunities for youth
- Leadership involvement from deacons
- Involvement in community and missions
- Increase in ministry resources
- Ongoing training and development
- Invite outside speakers

Once you know your goals, you must establish your objectives in an effort to accomplish them. You have to know where you are going. A famous quote we often hear is, *"If you fail to plan, you might as well plan to fail."* This is so true. You should have your mind made up that you are going to accomplish what you have set out to do. Your mind must be fixed on executing the plans that you have put in place.

There is a great Bible story about a Hebrew servant named Daniel who was taken to Babylon to serve and train for three years under Babylonian regulations. He was provided a delectable meal from the king's table that included ribeye steak and the finest wine. The Bible says in Daniel 1:8, "Daniel purposed in his heart that he would not defile himself with the portion of the kings meat or wine."

Because of his commitment to God's laws, he made up his mind not to partake and was willing to pay the consequences. Fix your mind and stick to what God has planned for you and the ministry. Remember, God always honors intentional planning, especially if it's kingdom planning for His glory and the good of others.

Second, you must become *inviting.* When I say inviting, I am talking about welcoming. Develop a culture that is welcoming. New leaders seek to serve young people in environments that are appealing and congenial opposed to chaotic and unfriendly. Young people desire churches where warmth and friendliness abide.

An inviting environment makes learning conducive for teaching and receiving the Word of God. Many youth ministries fail in this area causing members and non-members to abstain from attending the church.

2. *It Takes PARTNERING*
   Ecclesiates 4:9 says "Two are better than one for they can help each other succeed." This Bible verse helps us to see that we benefit as believers when we work in collaboration with others and and not in isolation. You cannot accomplish a lot on your own. However, when you partner up with an individual or a team you will increase your chances of better success. It is going to take the involvment of others in ministry for success to take place and keep the ministry from crumbling. Others leaders in the ministry must become stakeholders in the planning.

   Stakeholders are church leaders, children and youth workers, parents and even young people in middle or high school who can assist with bringing your goals to reality. Don't pattern yourself after

Spiderman or Superman! Follow the model of Batman who worked with Robin, the Lone Ranger who worked with Tonto and Green Hornet who worked with Kato.

It's amazing to watch the Superheroes work together. What about Black Panther? Wasn't it amazing to see how his family and team worked together to save Wakanda? They accomplished great success working together as a team. Sarah MacLean penned these words, "The best partnerships aren't dependent on a mere common goal, but on a shared path of equality, desire and no small amount of passion." I really like the end of her quote (*no small amount passion*). Passion is a burning desire to succeed. And that's what it takes to obtain success in ministry.

When you have two like-minded people with a desire to please God and build His kingdom, your ministry will withstand the test of time and not crumble. Discover like-minded people who are passionate about seeing young people saved and growing in their relationship with the Lord. Establish a time for fasting and praying so that you and your partner(s) can stand strong with resiliency and efficiency as you collaborate in ministering to young people.

3. *It Takes PROBLEMS*

Mark 2:3-5, tells the story of a lame man who was unable to walk. His four friends were able to get him to Jesus. When they arrived at the place where Jesus was ministering, they were unable to get into the crowded house. That was a problem. Yet, they did not allow this problem to stop them. They decided to go to Home Depot and purchase some equipment. They returned to the crowded house and without permission, they marched up to the top of the house and cut a hole in the roof and lowered the ill man to Jesus. The Bible says when Jesus saw their faith, he said to the man, "Your sins are forgiven."

Problems can be obstacles that turn into hurdles of victory. Problems can be questions of uncertainity that turn into answers of clarity. Don't allow problems to discourage or defeat you! God can take your challenges and use them as means of getting your breakthrough. James Dyson said, "Life is a mountain of solveable problems and I enjoy that."

Never forget that problems stimulate growth and something good can come out of a problem. Problems create dependence on God. Remember "Big Momma" use to say, "If I never had a problem, I would not know that God could solve it." So don't run from the problems, challenges or obstacles, confront them in a godly and biblical way. Remember, when it is about God, He will see you through.

Problems force evaluation. Problems cause us to face reality. We should look at our approaches, methods, motives and moods as to why we do what we are doing. Remember, don't fight, just embrace the predicament and trust God through faith that He will resolve it for His glory and the building of His kingdom.

4. *It Takes PEACE*

Colossians 3:15 says, "Let the peace that comes from Christ rule in your hearts." For as members of one body, you are called to live in peace. And always be thankful." (NLT) This is one of my favorite Bible verses in the book of Colossians. Paul is speaking to the Colossian church. He is reminding them of the peace that should permeate in them as believers. Peace is a state of mutual harmony between individuals or groups of people. Peace is the absence of chaos and confusion. A ministry filled with peace and harmony stabilizes the context for sustainable growth. Young people, workers and ministry leaders enjoy coming to a place of pacification.

Become intentional about creating a harmonious environment so that ministries are executed without drama. Young people have enough drama in their lives at home and school. They should not have to subject themselves to a youth ministry or church where continual discord and disharmony abides.

Strive for unity in the Spirit. This comes about through fervent praying and sincere humility. Sometimes, it's chaotic in youth ministry. Examples are: leadership is not on one accord, there is very little support from the pastor and deacons and you have a small budget (if any) for resources and materials.

Another one of my favorite Bible verses is from the Old Testament and is found in Isaiah 26:3. "He will keep you in perfect peace all those who trust in him and whose thoughts are fixed on him. (NLT)" Keep your mind fixed on God. Apply the biblical prinicples to your life. Walk in righteousness and watch God take care of everything else. Remember you can only account for yourself. If you are the peace maker in the ministry, don't abandon the ship. The young people need you! Stay PRAYED up in your devotional life. Stay READ up in your daily Bible reading (Quiet Time).

5. *It Takes PATIENCE*

In Psalms 40:1 David said, "I waited patiently for the Lord to help me, and he turned to me and heard my cry." What a powerful declaration! If we learn to wait on God, He will accomplish something great through us. David had a lot going on in his life. He searched for answers about his future, his family and his kingdom. What is patience? Patience is the ability to wait until something happens. What a great definition for patience. We all know that change does not take place overnight! It's a process and it can become extremely long or short. We must exercise patience. Every ministry is different. Every ministry's mission, vision and priorities are different.

Realize that your church may not choose to promote and enhance the Children and Youth Ministry the way you would like. Try not to get discouraged. Trust God and hear what He has to say! Take small steps toward the big steps. The second part of the Psalms 40:1b says "... and he turned to me and heard my cry." God will hear you! Heaven is recording your request. Just WAIT for heaven's response. Remember, Rome was not built in a day! Your ministry will not change in a day! Waiting for change in the ministry can produce stress. The stress is your test to trust God. The stress is your test to go deeper into your ability to depend on God, knowing He will handle everything in his timing. Unfortunately, patience is a process that is accomplished through waiting. A wise person once said "Patience is not the ability to wait, but the ability to keep a good attitude while waiting." What is your disposition while waiting on God to move?

Can others in the ministry detect your frustration? Are you wearing your dissatisfaction on your sleeves? Are you speaking out and perhaps creating a negative or divisive spirit in the church? God hears and sees what you feel and go through. He is not absent from what's going on inside of us! Trust the process of waiting on God. He knows the best course of action and He knows the beginning and the ending. Grandma used to say "He may not come when you want Him, but He is always on time." The ministry does not have to crumble while you wait. Just trust in God.

6. *It Takes POWER*

Acts 1:8a says, "And you shall receive power after the Holy Ghost has come upon you..." If you are to keep your ministries from crumbling, it will take the power of the Holy Spirit. These words were from Jesus himself. His words were meant for his disciples and followers. It is impossible to do ministry of any kind without the power of God! Simply put, it is the Holy Spirit that sustains and maintains us to minister to children and youth. Without His power for Children and Youth Ministry, we are useless! Mary McCloud Bethune penned these words, "We have a powerful potential in our youth, and we must have the courage to change old ideas and practices so that we may direct their power toward good ends." It truly takes God's power for us to change old habits and practices. Many of our ministries are crumbling because of obstinate attitudes and argumentative ways.

Our mission is to see young people accept Christ and begin to grow in their relationship with Him. However, sometimes our will and ways are not intentionally submitting to the Holy Spirit. The Holy Spirit desires to intervene and disrupt our way of doing things and inspire us with fresh and creative avenues for reaching children and youth. We must succumb to the leadership and direction of the Holy Spirit. How do we receive His power? Through intentional and humble submission. Remember Big Submission equals Big Power; Little Submission equals Little Power; No Submission, No Power. The power you receive from God is totally up to you!

7. *It Takes PERSISTENCE*

I Corinthians 15:58 says, "Be ye steadfast unmoveable always abounding in the work of the Lord for your labour is not in vain." Paul encourages the Corinthians to stay steadfast; not to give in or give up in their faith or the ministry. Children and youth leaders need stickability in order to successfully work with young people. You cannot be here today and gone tomorrow. Young people need to know you are there for the long haul, especially during their trials and tribulations. They need permanent fixtures in their lives to help them endure the temptations, trials and tribulations they encounter. That means you must consistently stay connected and involved with your young people.

Tell yourself, "A setback is not defeat!" Don't allow anyone or anything to hinder you from what God is calling you to do. You and your commmitment are there for their growth and development. If you are a pillar and you crumble, you can only imagine what will happen to the youth and the ministry. I like the second part of I Corinthians 15:58 "...for your labor is not in vain." It is reassuring to know that what we do for Christ will last. It is reassuring to know that what we do for the kingdom is not ineffectual or unsuccessful, but it has real value and significance. So don't give up or give in when things don't look right or feel right. Just because we don't see the seeds growing does not mean they have not taken root and are not growing. Push on by faith when you can't see the results. Move forward by faith when ministry does not model what you expect. Keep your hopes and energy levels high knowing we have a God who knows and sees all. Don't forget the powerful words of singer Dottie Peoples, "He's an on time God. Yes He is!" I truly agree with her!

Chapter Reflection

What was the most important thing that God spoke to you?

_____

_____

_____

_____

_____

_____

What did God speak to you about that you would like to implement in the next 30 to 90 days?

_____

_____

_____

_____

_____

_____

What would hinder you from implementing what God has spoken to you in this chapter?

_____

_____

_____

_____

_____

_____

_____

Keeping the Ministry from Crumbling

1. What are some things that can cause your ministry to crumble?

_____

_____

2. What are your plans for keeping your minstry from crumbling?

_____

_____

3. Who can you collaborate with in ministry?

_____

_____

4. How do people help to keep the ministry from crumbling?

_____

_____

5. How does Psalms 40:1 help you to keep the ministry from crumbling?

_____

_____

6. How can I Corinthians 15:58 encourage you not to give up?

_____

_____

Chapter Notes

Chapter 3

Using Outreach to Build the Ministry

"Here I am. Send me."
Isaiah

An important piece to Children and Youth Ministry is outreach. Outreach is instrumental in the growth of our young people. Engaging young people in outreach creates a valuable experience for them and exposes them to reaching outside of themselves. A youth ministry with a viable outreach program will ensure spiritual growth in the children and youth of the church.

The Definition of Outreach

When I think about outreach, I think about three simple definitions. First, outreach is reaching out to others outside of the four walls of the church. Second, outreach is the ability to go beyond your comfort zone. Third, outreach is the art of going out to bless others. Engaging young people in outreach is taking them beyond what they are accustomed. We must look for meaningful opportunities and experiences that connect our youth with outreach.

The Discipline Needed for Outreach

There are several disciplines needed in order to help our youth become successful in outreach. These disciplines are geared toward us as leaders as we seek to prepare our youth for outreach. I believe there are five initiatives we must employ in order for outreach to take place.

First, we must become *intentional*. Leaders should intentionally take ownership in seeing that outreach is not overlooked or missed. Reaching out is not something most young people are concerned about. It is not high on their priority list. Therefore, adult leaders must ensure that outreach with youth is not ignored.

Second, we must become *relational*. It's important to understand that the relationships we build with our youth will determine the number of students who become involved in outreach. Building significant relationships with young people make it easier to get them involved. Remember, outreach is not a priority for most of them. However, through the power of relationships, youth will involve themselves in outreach with other adult leaders.

Third, we must be *conversational*. Try having genuine, meaningful dialogue with young people by soliciting their ideas and input. Listen to their suggestions and ask them what they would like to do for outreach projects. Sometimes, their ideas are great ones. Allowing young people opportunities to share suggestions for outreach endeavors gives them a sense of ownership. Once they feel ownership at the beginning of the project, believe me, they will want to help implement and see it through.

Fourth, we must be *informational*. Activities and projects should provide learning opportunities. Our youth should be well informed about problems that plague our community as well as how they can help combat those problems through service. Make sure the outreach activity meets a need in your church or community.

Fifth, we must be *practical*. Know the scope of ministry you desire to do in outreach. Make sure it is within the context of your church's mission and vision. Don't bite off more than you can chew. It is easier and better to take baby steps and be successful than to take large steps and feel like a failure.

The Destination of Outreach

When I talk about the destination of outreach, I am referring to the end results of engaging our young people in outreach. What is it that we desire to see happen at the conclusion of the day?

First, connecting with young people is a destination of outreach to young people. To connect with young people is to be joined to them or to unite with them. Adult leaders must see ministry outside of the four walls of the church as an opportunity to hang out with the young people. It's crucial for us to get to know them and vice versa. Sometimes we need to "chill" with young people outside of the church to know what they are really like.

Second, challenging young people is a destination for outreach to young people. Involving young people in outreach challenges their faith. Seeing them step outside of their comfort zone to minister to others helps mature their faith. Young people need to be challenged to move from the comfortable to the uncomfortable. Outreach ministries give them that opportunity.

Third, confirming young people is a destination of outreach to young people. To confirm something is to make stronger or strengthen. It is our goal that young people become stronger individuals as a result of getting involved in outreach.

Fourth, committing young people to God is a destination of outreach to young people. Adult leaders' number one goal should be to see young people's lives changed and committed to God. As we pray and engage young people in mission, we should see God changing the hearts of students from the world to the Word and from the carnal to the spiritual.

The Decision of Outreach

Listed below are a variety of ideas children and youth can participate in while doing outreach. You can implement these activities monthly, bi-monthly, quarterly or yearly. You must decide what works best for your context. Children and youth can collaborate together and execute these activities or they can do them separately. The size of your ministry and the number of volunteers determines what's most doable for your ministry. Here are some outreach activities that have proven to be successful for me while in youth ministry.

- Assisting with Thanksgiving Baskets
- Collecting food and clothes for homeless
- Donating new or gently used books
- Establishing a shoe drive
- Evangelizing in the community

- Driving by and praying for people
- Distributing food to the needy
- Going Christmas caroling to sick and shut in
- Inviting people to church
- Laying hands on schools, clubs and strip clubs
- Making and distributing lunches for the homeless
- Participating in a community and church clean up
- Painting a senior's or needy person's home
- Passing out Bible tracts in the community
- Peer tutoring younger people by older youth
- Praying at flag poles at government buildings, jails, etc
- Raking leaves for seniors in the church
- Serving during the holidays with the Angel Tree and toy collection
- Visiting a nursing home
- Volunteering to help with Halloween activities
- Working at a shelter or food pantry
- Writing letters to military or college students

Debriefing after Outreach

It is vital to engage in a debriefing after serving in a mission activity. Looking at the challenges and celebrating the positives is always good for the debrief. Discuss what was good and what could have been done differently. Ask self-reflecting questions like, "How has this activity impacted you? What did I learn from the activity? How did it develop my spiritual growth?" Always close out with a word of prayer, thanking God for the experience of being able to make a difference in the lives of other people. Afterwards, begin looking for the next mission activity.

Chapter Reflection

What was the most important thing that God spoke to you?

_____

_____

_____

_____

_____

_____

_____

What did God speak to you about that you would like to implement in the next 30 to 90 days?

_____

_____

_____

_____

_____

_____

What would hinder you from implementing what God has spoken to you in this chapter?

_____

_____

_____

_____

_____

_____

Using Outreach to Build Ministry

1. Can you list two definitions for outreach?

   _____

   _____

   _____

   _____

   _____

2. Can you list some disciplines needed for outreach?

   _____

   _____

   _____

   _____

   _____

3. What are some destinations of outreach?

   _____

   _____

   _____

   _____

4. List some outreach activities from the book.

   _____

   _____

   _____

   _____

5. Which (3) activities are most doable for your ministry?

_____
_____
_____
_____
_____

6. What is debriefing?

_____
_____
_____
_____
_____

7. Why is it good to debrief after an outreach activity?

_____
_____
_____
_____
_____
_____
_____
_____
_____
_____
_____
_____

Dr. Kevin B. Lee

Chapter Notes

_____

_____

_____

_____

_____

_____

_____

_____

_____

_____

_____

_____

_____

_____

_____

_____

_____

_____

_____

_____

_____

_____

_____

_____

_____

_____

Chapter 4

Recruiting Volunteers

"In recruiting, there are no good or bad experiences. Just learning experiences."
Author Unknown

One of the things most needed, but seldom found in Children and Youth Ministry, is a surplus of volunteers. How do you find volunteers to work with today's children and youth? Better yet, how do you get the right volunteers to commit? You don't want just any volunteer. You should desire volunteers who are willing to invest time, talents, gifts and their hearts into the lives of children and youth. How do you find volunteers who have a passion for working with youth? Are there any such people out there? Absolutely! No matter what type of church you are in, small or big, conservative or traditional, urban or rural, there are proven ways to recruit volunteers.

One great way to get a hint on how to recruit ministry workers is to look at the "Recruiter of all Recruiters". He is Jesus Christ. Jesus recruited twelve, if not more, committed volunteers who, in turn, recruited others. Let's look at Jesus as our example and examine how He recruited His disciples.

1. Jesus' Observation of Potential Leaders

Matthew 4:18 says, "As Jesus was walking beside the Sea of Galilee, He saw two brothers – Simon, called Peter, and his brother Andrew. They were casting a net into the lake, for they were fishermen." Notice the verse says he saw! After Jesus' call to ministry, He started looking for the men who would help him build the kingdom. Jesus knew He needed help right away. After preaching and teaching in verse 17, we find Him looking for volunteers in verse 18. Jesus is watching and looking for leaders to train and develop for the next three years. As leaders, we must look out and look around for volunteers to help us build the kingdom!

We often say, "If God gives you a purpose, He'll make the provision." Look and keep looking. Verse 21 says, "When He had gone a little further He saw two other brothers..." He did not stop looking for leaders even when He had leaders. If God has assigned you to Children and Youth

Ministry, He will not leave you out there to do the work alone. He will provide.

A part of observation includes allowing potential leaders to come and observe you. This makes a wonderfully soft entry for someone who may be hesitant to jump in with both feet. However, there is a strong possibility that if they come for a few weeks and just observe, you will increase the likelihood of them committing.

2. **Jesus' Invitation to Potential Leaders**

Matthew 4:19 says, "And Jesus said unto them, follow me, and I will make you fishers of men." Jesus invites Andrew and his brother Peter to join Him in becoming fishers of men. What an invitation! Later on, in verse 21, Jesus extended an invitation to brothers James and John. They all accepted their invitation and joined Jesus in a three-year training program.

The Bible says in James 4:2, "You have not because you ask not." Sometimes, we are guilty of not getting help because we are waiting for someone to volunteer. We're caught saying, "I'm not going to beg nobody." Often, others are waiting for you to just ask. We're the ones who need help. Why wouldn't we then ask for it? Jesus did. Now, of course, Jesus didn't need help.

He actually wanted to enhance their lives and so do you. So, maybe just giving a simple invitation will not only help you help your children and youth but also help the one God has led you to. Personal invitations always go a long way. It shows you care and that you think they have what it takes to make a difference. In the process, you get an opportunity to cast the vision for your ministry.

3. **Jesus' Presentation to Potential Leaders**

In Matthew 4:19, Jesus said to the brothers , "I will make you fishers of men." He gave them something to look forward to as a result of working in ministry. When you engage others with an invitation, make sure to follow it up with a commercial. Yes, I said a commercial. You are advertising. You are making a presentation. People want to know what they can get out of volunteering. Be honest. Don't tell them all the children will like you. Don't tell them it will be the easiest volunteer opportunity you've ever had because both of those things are untrue and you know it. Instead, share with them how it has affected your life. Give a testimony of what God has done for you because of your service to children and youth. Share any information you can think of that will help them to see the ministry in the same manner you see it.

4. Jesus' Investigation of Potential Leaders

In Luke's account of Christ choosing his disciples, Luke 5:3a says, "And he entered into one of the ships, which was Simon's." Jesus actually entered into Simon's ship. What does this mean? Jesus intentionally got close to them perhaps to investigate the leaders he was interested in recruiting. If you have leaders in mind and you are trying to invite and convince them to join the ministry, you have to invest some of yourself during this process. People desire meaningful relationships. Jesus was relational. You must be relational. No one wants to work closely with someone in ministry who is not friendly, inviting and accepting. Remember, while you are investigating them, they are also investigating you and the ministry.

5. Jesus' Supplication for Potential Leaders

Luke 6:12-13 is a powerful passage of scripture that shows us just how great a leader and recruiter Christ was. It says, "And it came to pass in those days, that He went out into a mountain to pray. He continued all night in prayer to God. 13) And when it was day, He called unto Him his disciples: and of them He chose twelve, whom also He named apostles." Wow! Right before Jesus called His twelve disciples who would become the apostles, He isolated Himself and prayed all night. As soon as daylight came, then and only then, He chose His twelve. Could it possibly suggest that we might have more success in recruiting if we first spent some time in prayer? I'm not saying that we have to be like Jesus and pray all night. (Although it wouldn't hurt.) I am saying that such an important decision definitely deserves for us to fervently pray before we choose leaders.

Ways to Recruit Ministry Workers

Having effective adult leadership is essential to Children and Youth Ministry. Without support, a Children and Youth Ministry worker can get burned out quickly. Unfortunately, not every worker is as effective as they should be. How do you turn an ineffective worker into a superstar? Is that even possible? How do you recruit new talent to come and support and assist when most are so busy or so stretched already? How do you capture the passion and affection desired with the volunteers you have? Here are some suggestions:

1. Be Specific

What does the job entail? No one should be asked to do a job without a detailed description of what is asked of them. I suggest a job description. Many times, we are so desperate for volunteers,we are afraid that we might scare them off. Volunteers deserve to know what constitutes success even if it is an unpaid position. For example, if you want a volunteer to call youth once a week, then list it in the job description. If you need a volunteer to show up 30 minutes before Bible Study, make sure it is stated in some type of written format.

Volunteers don't necessarily mind bringing snacks. But they will want to know up front that it's part of the commitment. You get the idea! It is unfair to ask someone to join your ministry without providing them with full details so that they can make a sound decision. Believe it or not, this also helps you retain workers. When people know exactly what they are getting, they tend to be more content. Have you ever been asked to do something only to find out that it is taking more time than you were led to believe? Frustrating, wasn't it? Make sure you let volunteers know there is a background check that may require out-of-pocket expenses. The bottom line is that volunteers are more likely to commit when they know exactly what is expected.

2. Be Successful

If I asked you what makes a successful youth ministry, what would you say? Would your response be a certain number of participants? Fulfilling God's purpose? Is it to have an awesome worship service? No matter how you answer that question, you are actually right. Success is what you decide it is. You set the parameters on whether your ministry is a success or not. I think the most important indication of whether your ministry is successful boils down to these questions. Do my children and youth know who Christ is and who they are in Christ? Are they developing a growing relationship with Christ? It takes the right leaders to make sure this is accomplished. To recruit great leaders, it will take recruiting in the following way:

• Recruiting from the Front

One of the first things you need to accomplish is to cast the vision. First know and be clear of your vision. The Word of God tells us to write down the vision. Volunteers cannot get excited about your ministry unless they are offered practical literature with information about working with our children and youth. If the vision is written, you are communicating the vision and empowering your volunteers to be effective on the front end.

Start by creating success for ministry workers early. Refrain from placing new volunteers into situations that may be beyond their capability. This works to discourage more than encourage and results in them saying no or quitting at the most inopportune time. Volunteers who experience early success will have a better impression on the ministry and will be more likely to stay. You might want to consider starting ministry workers out with activities that are not intimidating. Allowing your volunteers to experience small successes can work wonders. You can slowly introduce them to more challenging and larger opportunities to serve.

Once volunteers start to become interested, be sure to place leaders in their area of passion. Don't force volunteers to work in an area in which they are not comfortable. That's a huge mistake! Talk with them and find out where their skills lie. Find out their interests. Listen to them. Allow them to be indecisive. Be okay with them not being sure about their area of ministry or even whether they want to work with your ministry. Invite them to come and observe prior to making a commitment. When they do make a decision, process their paperwork quickly. There is nothing that takes the wind out of the sail of a volunteer more than waiting for ministry paperwork to be completed.

- **Recruiting from the Middle**

So, now that you have your eager volunteers, you're happy! The ministry is going well. Volunteers are on fire. Now you can sit back and relax. Right? Absolutely not! You are still recruiting. You NEVER stop recruiting! Ministry workers, no matter how dedicated, leave. Things happen, schedules change, available times shift and passions decrease. So, you must always be prepared to lose a volunteer. However, the other side of that coin is what you do to retain the ministry workers you already have.

Support your volunteers by observing their classes and events. Be an objective participant. Put on clear glasses so you can see the ministry as strangers see them. Leaders need to know you're watching them. They need to know you inspect what you expect. Offer feedback and confront problems early. A great misconception is that you cannot have standards for volunteers. But you must! This helps you determine the coaching, training and retraining needed. If you find a deficit, team-teach for a few weeks or ask one of your former ministry leaders to come back just to train. They may not be interested in working with the ministry any longer. Don't just allow your great workers to leave without at least asking them to come back for training. With proper training, new teachers are more likely to experience success early.

- **Recruiting from the End**

How do you recruit on the back end? Create Action Programs. Establish clear outcome(s). What is your plan setting out to achieve? There may be multiple outcomes in which actions will contribute. You may wish to also establish dates or other metrics to assist in validation whether the outcome is achieved or not. Next, identify the stakeholders. Who is involved and what is their role? This could be as simple as clarifying those responsible, consulted or informed. Last, define actions/tasks. Each should have a due date, one owner, a description and a unique identifier. Depending upon the complexity, you may want to extend your simple list into groupings of activities rolled up to outcomes.

- Allow volunteers to move on
- Develop a 3/6/12 month plan
- Evaluate quarterly or as much as possible

- Host conferences and seminars/webinars

3. Be Supportive

The worst thing you can do is recruit volunteers, hand them a curriculum without training and resources, and then tell them you'll see them at the next meeting. To operate in excellence, leaders need training and encouragement. Please don't beg them to join your ministry and then leave them isolated in the world of teens and their cell phones. Orientate, train and set standards. Then, you have to regularly check in with them. This is important in their first 30 to 60 days. This is when they have the most questions and need the most direction.

- Discover the passions of your volunteers
- Create an environment of encouragement
- Give positive reinforcement
- Value your volunteers

4. Be Stretched

Why seek to stretch your volunteers? It can help them and you. As much as God has given them to you, He has also given you to them. Never forget this. You know personally how valuable working in ministry can be. You need to share your own passion with them. Volunteers are people and people often times get in a rut and get bored with their everyday lives. Working in the Children and Youth Ministry can help to give them a new outlook. Maybe they will learn something new and get excited about investing their time into the young people in your ministry. Their place of employment is not the only place volunteers can be professionally developed. Volunteering can increase knowledge in unknown areas as well as reignite and spark volunteers and get them excited. They may even find professional connections that can prove to be advantageous.

5. Be Sincere

Volunteers are looking for ministries that are genuine in seeking to impact and change the lives of young people. Steer away from any form of deceit or hypocrisy that can hinder volunteers from signing up. New volunteers expect the leadership to operate forthrightly and to be aboveboard while working with them. With new recruits, conceptualize your vision, passion and sincerity. It will motivate them.

Chapter Reflection

What was the most important thing that God spoke to you?

_____

_____

_____

_____

_____

_____

_____

What did God speak to you about that you would like to implement in the next 30 to 90 days?

_____

_____

_____

_____

_____

_____

What would hinder you from implementing what God spoke to you in this chapter?

_____

_____

_____

_____

_____

Recruiting Volunteers

1. Who is our key example in recruiting volunteers?

   _____

2. What was Jesus' first approach in recruiting volunteers?

   _____

   _____

   _____

3. Who were Jesus' first volunteers?

   _____

   _____

   _____

4. What's the best way to invite people to become volunteers?

   _____

   _____

   _____

5. What should be a part of your presentation?

   _____

   _____

   _____

   _____

   _____

6. Why is supplication so important in recruiting volunteers?

_____

_____

_____

_____

7. Can you list suggestions for recruiting volunteers?

_____

_____

_____

_____

8. Which suggestion is most impactful for you?

_____

_____

_____

_____

9. Why is it important to be supportive?

_____

_____

_____

_____

_____

_____

Chapter Notes

Chapter 5

Retaining Volunteers

"Eighty percent of success is showing up."
Woody Allen

Now that you have your volunteers all lined up, how do you keep them excited and coming back? Often times, you must work just as hard to retain your volunteers as you do recruiting them. Here are some solutions to retaining volunteers in your ministry.

Learn to Appreciate
The Apostle Paul quoted these words in Philippians 1:3-5, "I thank my God in all my remembrance of you, always in every prayer of mine for you all making my prayer with joy, because of your partnership in the gospel from the first day until now." (CEV) Paul was giving thanks for the ministry of the Philippian church. They had been a blessing to the kingdom and he wanted to express his appreciation.

Likewise, in ministry we must learn to express thanks to our volunteers.

Years ago, Janet Jackson had a song called, "What Have You Done for Me Lately?" Everyone wants to be acknowledged for the things they do. To retain the workers in your ministry, you have to show appreciation to them. Ministry workers volunteer because they are interested in making a difference in the lives of the children and youth they serve. It's a job making sure ministry workers know they are appreciated.

Some of the ways to make this happen is to say "thank you" frequently. "Thank you" doesn't cost a dime. I'm surprised many people have such a difficult time saying it. Mother Teresa said these words "Kind words can be short and easy to speak. But their echoes are truly endless." The kind and positive words we speak go a long way. Below is a list of suggestions youth leaders can enact to show appreciation for their volunteers:

- Plan appreciation activities for your ministry workers.
- Hold an annual appreciation luncheon or dinner.
- Acknowledge ministry workers as often as possible verbally or with small gifts, awards or certificates.

- Constant praise and prayer. Pray <u>for</u> your ministry workers and pray <u>with</u> your ministry workers.
- Celebrate faithful workers when they transition out of the ministry.
- Form a welcoming committee to welcome new ministry workers to the ministry.
- Give Whoppers candy with this note: "Thanks for your whopper ideas!"
- Give a cookie cutter with a note: "Thank you for molding kids' lives."
- Give a seed packet with a note: "Wow! You're planting God's Word in young children's hearts!"
- Give a Mounds candy bar with this note: "You're making a mound of difference!"
- Give Life Saver candies with this note: "You're a real lifesaver."
- Give a bag of peanuts with this note: "We're nuts about you! Thanks for bringing your kids out of their shell."
- Give a pack of Starbursts with this note: "Thanks for being a burst of energy."
- Give them a Mr. Goodbar with this note: "Thanks for being good to our youth."
- Give a stuffed shape heart with this note: "Thanks for being the heart of this ministry."
- Give a candle with this note: "You light up the lives of our youth.

- Give a roll of scotch tape with this note: "Thanks for your transparency with our youth."
- Learn your volunteers intimately. Learn their names. Listen to them intently. Write personalized notes of appreciation.

If you want your volunteers to stay with you, it is imperative that you learn to appreciate them.

Learn to Duplicate
Exodus 18:14 says "When Moses' father-in-law saw all that Moses was doing for the people, he asked, What are you really accomplishing here? Why are you trying to do all this alone while everyone stands around you from morning till evening?" (NLT) Jethro, the father in-law of Moses, realized that Moses was quickly on his way to burnout! Moses needed to duplicate himself. Sometimes we have the same tendency as Moses to overwork ourselves.

Do you have superhero attributes and tendencies? Do you have passion out of this world to reach children and youth? The answer may be yes. However, you can't do it all by yourself. You must find and train certain volunteers who share the same characteristics, qualities and passion you possess. Remember, you were not called to ministry alone. I know sometimes you may feel that you can get more done by yourself.

There may be some truth in that. You can go a lot further in ministry when you are able to duplicate yourself in others. It is not always an easy test. It takes a lot of time, energy and patience. I remember a quote that has stayed with me down through the years, "Success without duplication is merely future failure in disguise." Please don't forget to DUPLICATE yourself!

Learn to Communicate

Ephesians 4:29 says, "Don't use foul or abusive language. Let everything you say be good and helpful, so that your words will be an encouragement to those who hear them." (NLT) Paul encourages the church in Ephesians to speak words that build up and not tear down. Communication is very important in retaining volunteers. Communication is simply dialogue or discussion between two or more people. Communication is the key that unlocks the unknown and clarifies understanding. Volunteers want to associate with a shared vision. That means we must communicate the mission and vision of the youth ministry. They want to know the expectations and requirements.

These things along with goals and objectives help to get everyone on one accord in the ministry. Listen to their feedback. It is always good to listen to what they have to say. Volunteers who feel ignored won't volunteer for long. Ask for their ideas, listen to their suggestions and always follow up. Meet monthly, bi-monthly or quarterly to ensure information is being passed down to everyone. Create group chats, emails and conference calls to keep the communication going. James Humes penned these words, "The art of communication is the language of leadership."

Learn to Educate

II Timothy 2:15 says, "Study to shew thyself approved unto God, a workman that needeth not to be ashamed, rightly dividing the word of truth." (KJV) The Apostle Paul talks about the need for studying of the Word. Volunteers deserve education. In others words, they need training. Provide them with the resources they need to be successful. Participate in quarterly training with your volunteers.

Have resources and as many supplies as possible ready and available for volunteers to use. Look for teachable people. I'd much rather have a person who is inexperienced and teachable than an "expert" who can't be taught. Education combined with inspiration and information can create transformation in the class room. Look for conferences and workshops that can provide effective training for your volunteers. Invite motivational speakers and people who are gifted to make presentations to your volunteers. Look for books and periodicals that are useful for volunteers to gleen information that can assist and elevate them in their serving. Malcom X quoted these words,

"Without education, you are not going anywhere in this world."

Learn to Delegate

Exodus 18:21, 22 says "But select from all the people some capable, honest men who fear God and hate bribes. Appoint them as leaders over groups of one thousand, one hundred, fifty, and ten. They should always be available to solve the people's common disputes, but have them bring the major cases to you. Let the leaders decide the smaller matters themselves. They will help you carry the load, making the task easier for you." (NLT) As mentioned earlier, Jethro, the father-in-law of Moses, encourages him to select capable people who can assist him in the work. As leaders, we must look for capable volunteers whom we can delegate responsibilities. Motown Record Executive Barry Gordy once said, "I have this hidden ability to find hidden talent in people that sometimes they don't know they have." We must learn to find hidden abilities in our volunteers and invite them to join us in building up young people.

Remember, value the time of your volunteers and don't overload them with work. Make sure you are spreading out the work load. Just like you need balance, they need balance also. Volunteers enjoy using their strengths for a good cause. Just don't overwork them. Determine where their gifts best fit in the ministry.

Learn to Evaluate

Matthew 25:19 says "After a long time, their master returned from his trip and called them to give an account of how they had used his money." (NLT) This is a story about when a master gave three of his servants bags of silver. They were giving according to their ability. He leaves for a season and returns to see how well they did with the silver he left them. The master was evaluating their work. Likewise, we must evaluate the work of the volunteers. Evaluation should be done based on predefined expectations and roles. Make sure you are gentle when evaluating your volunteers. Inform them of the purpose of the evaluation. The purpose of the evaluation is to sharpen them for the ministry so that young people can grow in their relationship with God. There are several tools you can use for evaluating your volunteers. You can utilize a formal or informal approach. You can use a checklist. You can use monitoring and observation. Whichever method you employ, keep written records of the evaluation and of tangible steps to take to either improve or find new and innovative ways to serve.

Learn To Celebrate

Exodus 15:20 says "Then Miriam the prophet, Aaron's sister, took a tambourine and led all the women as they played their tambourines and danced." (NLT) Miriam is celebrating the crossing over the

Red Sea and the deliverance from Pharoah's mighty army. The volunteers that help in the ministry need to be celebrated. They give selflessly of their time and talents to build the ministry. They provide such a valuable service that truly makes a difference. So why not take time and use resources to celebrate volunteers for their sacrifice? Three ways that you can celebrate your volunteers are:

- **Volunteer Appreciation Activity**

    Host a small reception or luncheon to recognize those that have labored with you for the entire year. Make it a themed event with decorations, gifts and most importantly, food. I don't know why food is such a critical part of most celebrations, but it is. It doesn't take much!

- **Volunteer Appreciation Awards**

    Whenever you have all your ministry workers together, utilize that time of having an audience to recognize their hard work and their dedication to your ministry. All it takes is an appreciation certificate or trophy, but it can go such a long way.

- **Shout it Out**

    Shout from the mountain top and let everyone in the ministry know about the wonderful children and youth volunteers that are in your church. There are also a lot of free or low cost ways to appreciate volunteers. Write a press release and send it to local papers or your church newsletter. Have young people write thank you letters. Design a social media campaign featuring your star volunteers. Singing the praises of your volunteers publically will let them know how much you appreciate them!

Learn to Motivate
Matthew 19:26 says, "But Jesus looked at them and said, With man this is impossible, but with God all things are possible." Jesus is speaking to His disciples and helping them to understand that with God, they can accomplish anything. This is a powerful scripture that will help motivate volunteers. I have often heard that motivating others is hard work. That statement is probably true. However, children and youth leaders can stimulate others to action. This can happen in several ways. Try some of these stimulators: feedback, rewards, recognition, conferences, time, free food and fun.

Positive feedback is a great motivator. Often, volunteers are discouraged and are on the verge of quitting. Personal thank you notes and emails are wonderful ways to inspire volunteers. Spend time with volunteers during your free time. Spending time with volunteers will help enormously with their morale and motivation. Get to know your ministry workers! The bottom line is this: They need to know you and you need to know them.

Learn to Elevate
Deuteronomy 34:9 says "Now Joshua son of Nun was full of the spirit of wisdom, for Moses had laid his hands on him. So the people of Israel obeyed him, doing just as the Lord had commanded Moses." (NLT) Joshua was elevated because of his faithfulness. Learn to promote those within the ministry. You know those that have been faithful. You know those whose commitment level is unwavering and you can truly depend on them. What a blessing to promote because of faithfulness.
In Matthew 9:37 Jesus said, "The harvest truly is plentiful, but the labourers are few." Don't take for granted the small core of devoted volunteers whose presence is always there. Be ready to elevate them to the next level of ministry or greater responsibilities in ministry.

Keys To Retaining VOLUNTEERS

Value their time and energy.

Observe their interactions with young people.

Look for ways to affirm and appreciate them.

Understand their needs and weaknesses.

<u>N</u>urture them in the Word of God.

<u>T</u>rain them with new concepts quarterly.

<u>E</u>nergize them as much as possible.

<u>E</u>ncourge them throughout the year.

<u>R</u>each them where they are.

<u>S</u>tretch them when necessary.

Volunteers are a blessing! Continue to pray and ask God to give you wisdom in how to retain volunteers in the ministry. Some seasons you will operate in overflow of volunteers and some seasons you will fall short. Remember the words of the Apostle Paul in I Corinthians 15:57, "Therefore, my dear brothers and sisters, stand firm. Let nothing move you. Always give yourselves fully to the work of the Lord, because you know that your labor in the Lord is not in vain." (NIT) *Selah*

Chapter Reflection

What was the most important thing that God spoke to you?

_____

_____

_____

_____

_____

_____

_____

What did God speak to you about that you would like to implement in the next 30 to 90 days?

_____

_____

_____

_____

_____

_____

What would hinder you from implementing what God spoke to you in this chapter?

_____

_____

_____

_____

_____

Retaining Volunteers

1. List at least six components for retaining volunteers.

   _____

   _____

   _____

2. Which two stand out the most for you?

   _____

   _____

   _____

3. Out of all of the suggestions to show appreciation to your leaders, which two can you implement immediately?

   _____

   _____

   _____

4. What hinders leaders from educating their volunteers?

   _____

   _____

   _____

5. Why is evaluating volunteers important?

   _____

   _____

   _____

6. How does proper communication encourage volunteers?

_____

_____

_____

7. Who in the ministry is ready for elevation?

_____

_____

_____

8. What did Moses do publicly for Joshua?

_____

_____

_____

9. Under the VOLUNTEER acronym, which two letters (words) are you doing currently?

_____

_____

_____

10. Under the VOLUNTEER acronym, which two letters (words) do you desire to start doing?

_____

_____

_____

_____

Chapter Notes

_____

_____

_____

_____

_____

_____

_____

_____

_____

_____

_____

_____

_____

_____

_____

_____

_____

_____

_____

_____

_____

_____

_____

_____

_____

_____

_____

I'M PUZZLED! Notes on Structuring a Children and Youth Ministry

_____

_____

_____

_____

_____

_____

_____

_____

_____

_____

_____

_____

_____

_____

_____

_____

_____

_____

_____

_____

_____

_____

_____

_____

_____

_____

I'M PUZZLED! Notes on Structuring a Children and Youth Ministry

_____

_____

_____

_____

_____

_____

_____

_____

_____

_____

_____

_____

_____

_____

_____

_____

_____

_____

_____

_____

_____

_____

_____

_____

_____

Dr. Kevin B. Lee

I'M PUZZLED! Notes on Structuring a Children and Youth Ministry

_____

_____

_____

_____

_____

_____

_____

_____

_____

_____

_____

_____

_____

_____

_____

_____

_____

_____

_____

_____

_____

_____

_____

_____

I'M PUZZLED! Notes on Structuring a Children and Youth Ministry

_____

_____

_____

_____

_____

_____

_____

_____

_____

_____

_____

_____

_____

_____

_____

_____

_____

_____

_____

_____

_____

_____

_____

_____

Dr. Kevin B. Lee

I'M PUZZLED! Notes on Structuring a Children and Youth Ministry

_____

_____

_____

_____

_____

_____

_____

_____

_____

_____

_____

_____

_____

_____

_____

_____

_____

_____

_____

_____

_____

_____

_____

_____

_____

_____

_____

_____

I'M PUZZLED! Notes on Structuring a Children and Youth Ministry

_____

_____

_____

_____

_____

_____

_____

_____

_____

_____

_____

_____

_____

_____

_____

_____

_____

_____

_____

_____

_____

_____

_____

_____

_____

_____

_____

_____

_____

Dr. Kevin B. Lee

I'M PUZZLED! Notes on Structuring a Children and Youth Ministry

_____

_____

_____

_____

_____

_____

_____

_____

_____

_____

_____

_____

_____

_____

_____

_____

_____

_____

_____

_____

_____

_____

_____

_____

_____

I'M PUZZLED! Notes on Structuring a Children and Youth Ministry

_____
_____
_____
_____
_____
_____
_____
_____
_____
_____
_____
_____
_____
_____
_____
_____
_____
_____
_____
_____
_____
_____
_____
_____
_____

I'M PUZZLED! Notes on Structuring a Children and Youth Ministry

_____

_____

_____

_____

_____

_____

_____

_____

_____

_____

_____

_____

_____

_____

_____

_____

_____

_____

_____

_____

_____

_____

_____

_____

I'M PUZZLED! Notes on Structuring a Children and Youth Ministry

_____

_____

_____

_____

_____

_____

_____

_____

_____

_____

_____

_____

_____

_____

_____

_____

_____

_____

_____

_____

_____

_____

_____

_____

Dr. Kevin B. Lee

I'M PUZZLED! Notes on Structuring a Children and Youth Ministry

_____

_____

_____

_____

_____

_____

_____

_____

_____

_____

_____

_____

_____

_____

_____

_____

_____

_____

_____

_____

_____

_____

_____

_____

_____

_____

I'M PUZZLED! Notes on Structuring a Children and Youth Ministry

_____

_____

_____

_____

_____

_____

_____

_____

_____

_____

_____

_____

_____

_____

_____

_____

_____

_____

_____

_____

_____

_____

_____

_____

_____

_____

I'M PUZZLED! Notes on Structuring a Children and Youth Ministry

_____

_____

_____

_____

_____

_____

_____

_____

_____

_____

_____

_____

_____

_____

_____

_____

_____

_____

_____

_____

_____

_____

_____

_____

_____

I'M PUZZLED! Notes on Structuring a Children and Youth Ministry

_____

_____

_____

_____

_____

_____

_____

_____

_____

_____

_____

_____

_____

_____

_____

_____

_____

_____

_____

_____

_____

_____

_____

_____

_____

_____

_____

Dr. Kevin B. Lee

I'M PUZZLED! Notes on Structuring a Children and Youth Ministry

_____

_____

_____

_____

_____

_____

_____

_____

_____

_____

_____

_____

_____

_____

_____

_____

_____

_____

_____

_____

_____

_____

_____

_____

_____

_____

_____

_____

I'M PUZZLED! Notes on Structuring a Children and Youth Ministry

_____

_____

_____

_____

_____

_____

_____

_____

_____

_____

_____

_____

_____

_____

_____

_____

_____

_____

_____

_____

_____

_____

_____

_____

_____

Dr. Kevin B. Lee

I'M PUZZLED! Notes on Structuring a Children and Youth Ministry

_____

_____

_____

_____

_____

_____

_____

_____

_____

_____

_____

_____

_____

_____

_____

_____

_____

_____

_____

_____

_____

_____

_____

_____

_____

_____

I'M PUZZLED! Notes on Structuring a Children and Youth Ministry

_____

_____

_____

_____

_____

_____

_____

_____

_____

_____

_____

_____

_____

_____

_____

_____

_____

_____

_____

_____

_____

_____

_____

_____

Dr. Kevin B. Lee

I'M PUZZLED! Notes on Structuring a Children and Youth Ministry

_____

_____

_____

_____

_____

_____

_____

_____

_____

_____

_____

_____

_____

_____

_____

_____

_____

_____

_____

_____

_____

_____

_____

_____

I'M PUZZLED! Notes on Structuring a Children and Youth Ministry

_____

_____

_____

_____

_____

_____

_____

_____

_____

_____

_____

_____

_____

_____

_____

_____

_____

_____

_____

_____

_____

_____

_____

_____

_____

I'M PUZZLED! Notes on Structuring a Children and Youth Ministry

_____

_____

_____

_____

_____

_____

_____

_____

_____

_____

_____

_____

_____

_____

_____

_____

_____

_____

_____

_____

_____

_____

_____

_____

_____

_____

I'M PUZZLED! Notes on Structuring a Children and Youth Ministry

_____

_____

_____

_____

_____

_____

_____

_____

_____

_____

_____

_____

_____

_____

_____

_____

_____

_____

_____

_____

_____

_____

_____

_____

Dr. Kevin B. Lee

I'M PUZZLED! Notes on Structuring a Children and Youth Ministry

_____

_____

_____

_____

_____

_____

_____

_____

_____

_____

_____

_____

_____

_____

_____

_____

_____

_____

_____

_____

_____

_____

_____

_____

_____

I'M PUZZLED! Notes on Structuring a Children and Youth Ministry

_____

_____

_____

_____

_____

_____

_____

_____

_____

_____

_____

_____

_____

_____

_____

_____

_____

_____

_____

_____

_____

_____

_____

_____

Dr. Kevin B. Lee

I'M PUZZLED! Notes on Structuring a Children and Youth Ministry

_____

_____

_____

_____

_____

_____

_____

_____

_____

_____

_____

_____

_____

_____

_____

_____

_____

_____

_____

_____

_____

_____

_____

_____

Products by Dr. Kevin B. Lee

Books
Volume 1 - *Putting the Pieces Together*
Volume 2 - *Making the Pieces Fit*
Volume 3 - *Teaching Pieces to the Puzzle*
Volume 4 - *Practical Pieces to the Puzzle*

Training Manuals
Building A Solid Youth Ministry

Training Manual #1 - Basic Training
Training Manual #2 - The Awards Goes To...
Training Manual #3 - Super Heroes Versus Villains
Training Manual #4 - Who Moved My Pieces

CDs Series for Training

Back to the Basics
Organizing Your Ministry
Building a Solid Children's Ministry

Developing Your Leaders
Qualities of an Effective Leader
The Frustrations of Youth Ministry

Teaching That Makes a Difference #1
Teaching Tips for Classroom Growth
What Every Teacher Should Know

Dr. Kevin B. Lee

For More Information or to Order Materials

KBL Ministries
770-879-8789

www.KevinBLee.org

kbleemin@aol.com

www.BereanGwinnett.org

www.BuildingASolidYouthMinistry.org

www.ingramcontent.com/pod-product-compliance
Lightning Source LLC
Chambersburg PA
CBHW060120050426
42448CB00010B/1956